WRITING OUR LIVES

Published by Diversity Arts Wales/Butetown History & Arts Centre Copyright © 2015 Butetown Arts & History Centre and the authors.

All rights reserved. This book or any portion thereof may not be reproduced or used in any manner whatsoever without the express written permission of the publisher except for the use of brief quotations in a book review or scholarly journal.

First Edition: 2015

ISBN 978-1-326-21824-9

Cover Art Copyright: Abeer Ameer

ACKNOWLEDGEMENTS

We would like to thank the Awards for All programme of the Big Lottery for supporting this project. Our warmest thanks also go to the Hayaat Women's Trust, Butetown History & Arts Centre and all participants and volunteers who have helped with various aspects of the project.

TABLE OF CONTENTS

Introduction   9

Home, Belonging, Tradition   11

Being Different   35

A Sense of Place   45

Identity, Womanhood, Connection   55

Advice   85

Memorable Moments & Objects   93

Belief   105

Grief & Loss   111

Writing   117

Contributor's Notes   127

Facilitator's Notes   130

INTRODUCTION

A few years ago, a young Somali writer, Nadifa Mohamed, came to Cardiff to do research for a novel about her father's life as a seafarer. Butetown History & Arts Centre had recently completed a rich and extensive oral history and photographic project on the life of Somali seamen and industrial workers. These resources informed Nadifa's successful novel, *Black Mamba Boy*, based on Somali life stories. In 2013, Zainab Nur from the Cardiff-based Hayaat Women's Trust came to Butetown History & Arts Centre with the idea of inviting Nadifa Mohamed to Cardiff to read from her work. From this initial idea we developed the *Writing Our Lives* project, a series of creative writing workshops which offered women from diverse backgrounds an opportunity to share their own life stories. The project was launched in May 2014 with a reading by Nadifa Nohamed in the Wales Millennium Centre from her second novel, *Orchard of the Lost Souls*. This book is the result of that process.

Cardiff has been a multi-ethnic city since the mid-nineteenth century. From the 1840s onwards Cardiff developed as major coal exporting port with a diverse population who had roots in Africa, the Middle and Far East, Europe and the Caribbean. The opening of the Suez Canal in 1869 saw many seafarers arrive from the Horn of Africa and Yemen. The Docks' and Tiger Bay communities that developed around the port were marked by ethnic and religious diversity and a mixing of races and cultures. Since the decline of Cardiff as port, new waves of migrant workers and refugees have come to settle in the city. The contributors to this book include women who grew up in Tiger Bay and the Docks as well as women who have come to Cardiff in more recent decades. The cross-generational and multi-faith aspects of the group have made the project particularly enriching.

As a group we worked with two tutors, Christina Thatcher and Emma Beynon, and met regularly over a period of nine months. Participants were encouraged to write freely about their experiences of childhood, growing up and adulthood using prompts as varied as objects, poetry and photographs to develop their writing skills and help capture the voices of their stories.

Together we arranged the work into themes so each section of this collection represents experiences from different British Black, Asian or Muslim women. Although we have included Contributor's Notes, each individual creative piece remains anonymous so the women could feel free to share writing about all of their experiences, including ones which they found difficult or revealing.

We hope that the life experiences that have produced this collection will help you better understand what it is like to live in an ethnically diverse and changing city. Above all we hope you will enjoy this anthology.

Home, Belonging, Tradition

Family Tradition

My recently widowed, ninety-year-old father-in-law is staying with us. He hasn't been the same since his wife passed away just before Christmas last year. It was quite sudden. He seems especially downbeat when he sees photos of her. Frequently, as if by some magic trick, he produces photos from his papers in his pockets, despite our best attempts to keep them hidden. He writes poetry addressing her with words of longing, telling of his pain, how she shouldn't have been the one to go first being fifteen years his junior. He laments that even the months of spring and summer seem like a dark, cold winter. He silently cries in his room. He tries to be a strong Iraqi man, stoic, but his eyes and voice frequently betray him. There is an Iraqi saying that I remember every time I see him: "Rather I live a year as a lonely bachelor, than endure one day as a widow". I see sorrow in his eyes and I hear it is his voice. I sense it when he breathes, like his whole existence as a widower is a struggle. Even to breathe.

My two sons, Yaseen aged ten and Besheer aged seven, were really devastated when their gran passed away. They had had a sleepover the night before at her house. My parents-in-law lived in a flat around the corner from our house, and the boys used to visit them daily. My mum said that my mother-in-law would have even given her eyes to her grandchildren, if they had asked.

When Yaseen would see his grandfather falling apart in the days following her death, he would go near him and lower his head. Jidoo (grandfather) Ahmed would kiss his head and smile.

Nowadays, my father-in-law (Jidoo Ahmed) wanders aimlessly around the house once he's finished reading and commentating on his newspapers. After noon, he asks me hourly when the boys will return from school. He always feels sorry for them being at school for such a large part of the day.

It is when the boys step in through the door that Jidoo's demeanour completely changes. There is a gleam in his eyes, he lights up when they come home and say "Salam" to him. He'll hum a little tune, which has rhythm enough for me to want to do a little jig, but I never do for fear of showing my own lack of rhythm. The only other time I notice an exhibition of happiness is when he sees that the newspaper has come in the morning. It's as if these moments are reminders that there is some sweetness in being alive.

When Yaseen and Besheer come into the house, they make a slight bow to my father-in-law so that he can kiss them on the head. He asks them how many kisses they would like; this usually varies between three and a thousand. After negotiations, if the number is rather high, he proceeds to kiss and counts them out in Arabic as he goes along. He then asks me how many kisses I would like on my head. I say five. He gives ten. If he's feeling particularly Western, he will count them out in English 1-2-3-4-5-6-7-8- 9-10.

Whenever he sees a pretty woman on the television he turns to my youngest, Besheer, or will sometimes call for him. He has a wide grin. He has never been one to laugh loud, but I hear a little chuckle, which is the closest thing to laughter I think he can do.

Sometimes he giggles to himself so much that he can't get the words out. He says to Besheer how he heard that Besheer is looking to get married and since the girl on of television is nice looking, if he fancies her, the family will go to her parents as a group and asked for her hand in marriage. Besheer says "not before my older brother" in broken Arabic. Each time it is pronounced differently, sometimes as swear words, but it's okay because Jidoo is hard of hearing. Jidoo always replies that there are no age limits to love so if Besheer is interested, he just needs to say the word. After lengthy protestations from Besheer, Jidoo agrees that maybe, at seven years, he is a bit young, so asks when he is thinking of getting married. Besheer asks me how to say "twenty years" in Arabic. I tell him and this becomes his regular answer.

One day, Besheer approaches me and indicates he wishes to speak privately. He whispers that he doesn't actually want to get married in twenty years and that it would ruin his plan to marry when he is eighty-seven years. I asked him why so late when he might want to have children and he'll need energy to play with them. He replies "Good. I don't want to have kids, they won't listen and I don't want to have to shout."

I tell him that this is not necessarily the case and they might actually might be really good listeners. He says that he and Yaseen are the best children in the world and they *never* listen. He then asked how to say one hundred years in Arabic and that is the end of that.

My Dad

Behind most successful women there's a supportive father – encouraging, not belittling, letting you know the world's your oyster. My Father was like that. We understood each other without words. There were no barriers, no "woman's place is in the home". I used to finish his sentences for him. I can understand now how irritating that must have been, suggesting he was predictable. It's just that I knew how his mind worked, and where he was going with a train of thought. Now my daughter does it to me.

I wasn't pressurised to do well at school – that came from me – but I was encouraged, consoled if things went badly, celebrated if they went well. A house with books leads to reading. We didn't have a telly 'til I was mid-teens. My parents thought it would destroy the family (and when they did get one it was hidden in a cabinet). We went to plays, opera, pantos, concerts and heard music on the huge radiogram, from Paul Robeson to Beethoven.

Dad didn't talk about growing up in Vienna, his escape from the Nazis, Mussolini's Italy, then safety in Britain. I wish I'd pushed him more. I got most of the stories from my Mother, and I'm not sure how true or accurate they were. My Father worked hard, loved us, loved his adopted home. On holidays he was the life and soul, at home often tired, alone.

Me

I have a culturally rich heritage, I am from a background of relative poverty which was rich in resourcefulness. The value of hard work and honesty were promoted at home. My grandfather showed me how to be patient and kind to others and to be adaptable in the face of adversity. To recognise the value and beauty of things, even when others no longer had any use for them. He made us a dolls' cradle out of recycled wood and taught me to tell the time on his pocket watch when I was seven.

I loved the fairy tale the *Red Shoes* and one day out of the blue I awoke to find a pair of my old shoes which he had painted red.

He often told me stories of how he stowed away on a ship from Barbados when he was fourteen and about his adventures at sea in the days of sailing ships. Grampy said that he was born with a caul (veiled membrane) on his face; this meant that he was able to see spirits and would never drown at sea.

During the war he was travelling in a convoy of ships and one night he was due on night watch. He didn't usually wear a life jacket and could not swim. He heard a voice saying "put on your Mae West jacket," so he sewed a button onto it and put it on. During the night a torpedo struck the middle of the ship and he was blasted into the sea, hitting his head on a piece of wood. He was in a coma for a long time and spent many months in hospital and was one of only two survivors.

My Aunt's Voice after Jonathan Edwards

It's the four foot six voice that helps me stand tall,
that sways to the songs.
It's the rhythmic serenade of old Iraqi ballads.
It's the voice that teased her little brother, my father, so.
My aunt's voice, those calm dulcet tones that smile
with each word.

It is the voice I wished to adopt as my own.
It is the voice I hear when I want to feel safe, the voice telling
stories filled with laughter.
It is the voice that shouts names of farmyard animals at the bad
drivers in Baghdad streets.
It is the voice that laughs even when angry,
It is the voice that pulls me up when gravity has overwhelmed
me.

It is the voice I yearn to hear when seeing her smile
in my mind's eye.
It is the voice that led banter on my wedding day.
It is the voice that accompanies the smile
that makes her eyes disappear.
It is the voice that comes with the soft hands
that hide the tiredness from work.

It is the voice that speaks the same love as her eyes.
It is the voice that tells me I am missed.
It is the voice that tells me ears love my laughter.
It is the voice that tells me my voice is loved.

How to Visit Home

Eat the refrigerator clean. Fish out the last exo from the jar.
Write neat lists. Dream about being there. Scrub the stove.
Leave the allotment key for El and the house key for Rose.
Watch the cool rain, and pack for summer heat:
a romper, a pair of red sandals.
Put all the houseplants into the bathtub.
Bathe them for the weeks alone.
Tell everyone here you can't wait to go home.
Leave in the dark, and count the blurred hours: black cab,
rocking coach, roaring plane, Dad's old Subaru rumbling
at the curb.
Arrive in the dark, in summer fog. Pour out your first news.
Drive north.
Marvel at the long highway, furred with spruce,
unscrolling for hours.
Breathe in: pine pitch, sea muck, shorn grass, red clover.
Soak up the crickets, count fireflies, swat mosquitoes, pick off
the ticks.
Sleep outside in the hayfields and foxgloves.
Swim in the bitter ocean; swim in the soft lakes.
Sleep in your old bed.
Tell your mother all the unsaid things. Have one real fight.
Eat cornbread, eat tomatoes from the garden, eat pizza on the
porch in a thunderstorm, eat at least one lobster roll.
Listen to your friends talk in the bluing dark. Count laughlines
around their eyes, fresh inches on their children,
blurred burgeoning ideas.
Catch their babies with your arms outstretched.

Do not expect them to finish their sentences.
Pack in so many visits you wear out your sandals.
 Dance in your sleeveless dress. Feast on late night Holy Donuts
at the wedding of a cousin.
Bring lemon sorbet with you, bring a six pack of dark beer,
bring proof of how you miss everyone.
Tell so many stories you wear out your news.
Feel far away, partial, a little different.
Have at least three good cries.
Drown yourself in corn on the cob, in maple syrup.
Then start to feel the pull of things
you should really be doing now.
Note the fat, oversized strip malls, the garish, dazed cars.
Crave ridge lines, cliff shores, tidy terraced houses,
your rhythms, your city.
Wonder about the state of the runner beans, your library books.
Wonder about your lists, your new friends,
the houseplants in the tub.
Tell everyone there you can't wait to go back.
Feel apart. Miss the rain. Go back.

Childhood Memories

Growing up in Bedfordshire for me was extremely difficult. My parents were quite introverted especially my mother, who didn't speak English very well. My father was most of the time at work. I feel I grew up too fast, as I felt responsible for my siblings taking care of them in-case they got bullied especially at school. I wasn't bullied at school but was called horrible names which put my confidence right back in deep waters. However, my sister was hit with a hockey stick across the face she ended up in a hospital. We were called all sorts of names. Abusive language was used quite often which put us right back into the black hole. Each time we've tried to take a positive step to go outside the front door people made you feel different. This made me feel inadequate and stupid, I found that very upsetting. But I really wanted to flourish and integrate, because of my parents' lack of input into my education which made it dire hard to make friends. I found my parents were colourless. I probably was looking through rose tinted glass.

I came into this world different, but my past experience moulds me easily into most kinds of situations. Anger and frustration leaves you in despair.

But I came into this world different to learn from others and it's a question of learning from experience believing in your own abilities and never, ever, give up. Appreciate differences and reflect on other peoples' views, learn to live and let live, to be unique, me.

Concrete Jungle

Its been years since I moved away from Ninian Park Road in Riverside. The landscape still remains the same, no trees, no parks, no greenery. The place where I lived has been knocked down and replaced by a bigger concrete structure. The pub has gone and in its place is an adventure playground. Yet still no trees. Each time I go down Ninian Park Road, I see things through different eyes. I notice the houses, still looking quite rough and I remember the infestation of mice which was normality for some of the residents on Ninian Park Road. I remember playing on the railway tracks. Yes it was happy times. Each family seemed to not have the means to be extravagant or excessive in either food, clothing or shelter. Except of course the adventures. Even though we were a street full of different cultures, religions and colours we were a community and most of us were in the same situation. I remember the Saturdays when there were football matches, the pub was full, the groups of rowdy men chanting for their teams, Cardiff City Supporters were dressed in blue. Living on top of a church and attending the church belonging the Pastor, who was a friend to my mother's landlord and soon to be step-father, and having a staunch, strict Jamaican, born-again Christian as a mother I remember, sometimes, me and my sisters having to (we had no choice) sing gospel songs and choruses to the passing crowds of football fans, who use to chant back at us 'all in pink, all in pink, didn't my finger stink'. To us having to sing was so embarrassing but in a way it was something to do, it was quite funny. I noticed that as I got older I became so embarrassed about partaking in 'open air' meetings. I never understood why we had to go out and sing when the noise of the football crowd would drown out our uncontrolled, out of tune songs. But when I look back, quite a few people came into the church because they heard us sing on a Saturday, so if our singing brought comfort, then the embarrassment was all for a good reason.

Coming Home

We landed, rain pouring just like home, the post boxes, uniforms the same, and smells everywhere, the same. The rain cleared and the sun came, but my first impression stayed the same… Cardiff home!

The people are so inviting, engaging in local banter with the children. There isn't a divide here, young, old, dreads, baldheads everyone seems connected, seems as one.

Everywhere we go, the bright sands of the golden beach and the blue, blue waves gently arriving one by one on the shore, just like the people!

Maybe it's a spell, a spell that everyone is under as soon as they touch the humid Island.

The smiles from everywhere entrap you into smiling back, you've caught it, too – you're under the spell of the land that heals, the land where all your troubles melt away by the sun.

The Island of Barbados where the sense of belonging is so, so strong.

Back home I question my children and friends: Was it a dream? But no, it wasn't, they feel the same!

Holiday Perspectives

Son 6

I play on the hot yellow sands and in the cool water. The sand slips through my fingers, I can't hold it tight, it squeezes through the gaps. When I'm so, so hot, boiling, I run and splash into the cool, calm, bright blue sea. I splash around and duck under water until I can no longer hold my breath. There's my brothers and sisters and people all around under the same spell. I'm aware someone's looking at me! We splash each other like we just knew it was the "right" thing to do. It's okay to talk to anyone here, I'm greeted by smiles. I'm a boy with long dreadlocks, back home I'm bullied and called a girl. Here there are whole families with dreads. They call after me "little brother? little youth?" It feels good, I belong.

Son 5

Massive pool, great big beach, amazing big burgers to eat. There is so much to do, everyone is happy! I dig a giant hole along with new friends, we work together all day and make a dam. A girl builds a castle. It's getting dark and the waves break through the dam into the moat crashing through the castle. Our day is complete.

Son 4

I can't leave my mum's side, I can't leave my mum's side, I don't know why, but I can't leave my mum's side. I follow mum on the beach, I follow mum into the sea, it's cold. I follow mum. Mum tries to distract me, but I'm not daft. She's telling me to dig, I love to dig, but I can't leave my mum's side, I can't leave my mum's side. I don't know why but I can't leave my mum's side.

Daughter 3

It's so hot here, I look so good in my new clothes, I look good in the pool and on the beach. I like the catamaran, it takes us to the other sides of the Island. The food and drinks are free and taste so delicious! It's the place to be.

Daughter 2

We get up in the morning and chill by the beach, we meet our friends and have tasty treats to eat. My brothers are occupied by digging in the sand. I take a good book and get entranced by the whole experience. It gets dark early, we go home and cook, before long we're so tired and put on a movie. We hear the wind pick up and loud pattering on the metal roof, faster and faster, a tropical storm has arrived. We jump into our beds and cover our ears with our blankets! Hoping for it to pass. We hear a loud roar of thunder, seconds later the lightening lights up the whole villa, hours later it's still thundering and surges of lightening seep through the windows. Total darkness, no power.

Daughter 1

We landed finally and after hours and hours of queuing in the stuffy airport, mum and the crew came to pick us up. After an eight and a half hour flight, my little sister and I were exhausted. It was such a delight to see my siblings, the villa was huge with a pool and it looked just like the pictures! Playing with my brothers that I had missed the last week was great, throwing them into the pool splashing each other, this is the best place to be.

Was it a Dream? Return to My Father's Land

My mother took me and my two siblings to Kashmir to my father's family home when we were kids. The house was like a farmhouse, it was surrounded by mountains and hills. We had banana trees, mango trees, and a plum tree; it was amazing. What really sticks out in my memory is that it had a fantastic lake with a gorgeous running ravine, you could see it during the day. At night, when it was all quiet and we were all tucked up in bed, you could hear water running through the ravine, it was so soothing that it would send you off to sleep.

During the day people would go for a swim in the lake. Some would do their laundry washing and even put it out to dry. There was a foot path that led to the other houses. Sometimes cattle would quench their thirst down by the river, in a special place just for them. We had an all-inclusive water well, that supplied water to our house. The view from the house was stunning, so amazing, everything seemed so big, it was overwhelming. It was awesome.

Adulthood

When I was young, I always thought that it would be great to leave home, to not have anyone to answer to and be treated as an adult. Just because you reach the age of 18, it does not necessarily mean you are an adult. My initiation into adulthood came at a time when I was not prepared for it. As a child/teenager I had been really spoilt by my sister. Housework, cooking and chores were alien to me. However, when I reached 18 I had to leave home due to a domestic dispute. Here I was alone and did not know what to do or where to go, but I believe that in situations where we find ourselves in complete despair and disarray, we have our own guardian angel. My guardian angel must have spoken, whispered in the ears and opened the love channels of the heart of a friend of my mother, and she offered me a place to stay as long as I wanted. In my heart I knew it would only be on a temporary basis. Here I was Homeless, no place to call my own, but I was thankful, I did not have to sleep in the street. The husband of my mum's friend eventually put me in contact with a friend of his who rented flats. So this is adulthood.

Being Useful

When she went home, after ten years, she knew where to find everything: white bog cedar from Downeast for the school gardens, black compost with shell and bone that made the pumpkins and melons jump, the best thrift stores, art supplies, and cider donuts. She knew where to go to pay a parking ticket, where to borrow a hacksaw, and where the purple grapes grew out of the parking lots in October. She knew where to go when someone said turn left where the Happy Wheels used to be, how to skip the traffic on Forest Ave, and how the mirrors in the old red movie theatre warped your face. She was twenty-five, a bird returning. She knew the place by heart.

The city was full of new occupants, all with their own ways. She knew its joints, its brickwork and history, its hidden swimming places, and learned some of the new ones. Ahmed told her about the fishing spots his father had found along the wharfs and the bridge to Falmouth that caught the flood and ebb tide, for example. On Saturdays at the crowded men's football league games, someone sold pupusas hot; it was Maria's mother. At the Sacred Heart cathedral in the East End, the Acholi grandmothers gathered on weekends for the funerals of friends. The museum where her own grandmother volunteered opened for free late on Fridays. There were lectures at the art school on Thursday evenings, but she was so tired at the end of her days outside that she fell asleep in the dark slideshows.

She rode her white bicycle everywhere in the same rubber and leather Beans boots her mother and grandmother wore. Over the years, she worked through three pairs. Eight miles to the farm. Three across town. Two to the big store for food. Seventeen home to take a bath in a clean tub and rinse off the city. Eleven to her grandmother's house for chicken salad sandwiches and the pine-shaded shared pool. For work, she drove a twenty-year-old sixteen-passenger green van packed with pitchforks and teenagers – and even, once, on the highway, a nanny goat and her kid. From the schools, she knew the names and faces of hundreds of moon-bright kids, and roomfuls and hallways of teenagers, each with his or her own style. She knew so many people in her small city that on Halloween, at three in the morning, when she complimented an astronaut walking down Cumberland Ave on his costume, he lifted his visor and called her by name. He'd been to kindergarten with her little brother. When people asked her for things she knew where to find them, who to ask, or how to make them. She felt in herself like a good, sturdy pitchfork: useful, full of purpose.

At first, she lived in Bayside with the punk collective, a mistake, where her housemates wore greasy bandanas and hosted bands with tattoos on their faces up from New Orleans. She cleaned the house after the bands went back to New Orleans, opening the windows to let out the smell of homemade fried chicken. She learned how to garden, how to gather a group of fifty in the rain, how to harvest squash leaves for Rwandan peanut stew, and how to coax a sour cherry tree to bloom. She learned how to cook the tiny, pink eggplants the way Iqbal's mother did it; she learned how to listen closely to all the teenage drama and not judge; she learned how to make things happen; she learned how to argue with the social worker that Fowzia was flunking out not because she slow but because she was depressed. She learned to let the hardest things, the bad days, the things that never seemed to change, rinse off of her in a hot shower.

She was so tired and happy after work sometimes she fell asleep face down on her bed, while it was still summer twilight. She moved up on the hill with her best friend after that, and they gathered around them a pack of strays, younger brothers between jobs and heartbroken friends. Two men came north chasing after them; to keep up, the two men came out to the farm, and did dishes in great steaming wash tubs out in the rain. They helped dig potatoes, build raised beds, muck out the pigs and the goats. The whip-thin one, newly bearded, worked the ache of long days out of her shoulders with his hands. Through the windows of their apartment, she knew the yellow quality of light that meant a summer sea fog that would burn off before noon, and the flat slate light that meant snow.

For Eid one year she went to Riverton to eat Fatima's chicken in her best dark blue dress, before Fatima got married and moved to upstate New York. She wore the same blue dress to Easter lunch at the club with her grandfather, gone now, then frail and regal in his silk paisley cravat. She wore it a third time for a first date to an outdoor summer concert with the man who moved north for her. That Eid, the rain was torrential, thunderous. That rail thin boyfriend, the one who moved north, the one she ended up marrying, wore a tie and shined his shoes. They picked up Will on the way, sixteen and massive in an ACDC teeshirt, with his worshipful little brother. Big, misanthropic Will, who drew unicorn comics, and tiny, forthright Fatima, who already had two jobs at eighteen, made for an unexpected friendship, but there you go. At Fatima's shining house with its scarlet curtains, the four white Americans perched on the sofas with plates heaped with chicken, rice, bisbas and sambusas, while Fatima's mother sat on the stairs, watching them eat with amusement, and listening to them talk. She had survived the war and the refugee camp and relocation to this cold place with three daughters and was still very beautiful.

'Fatima, ask them what our language sounds like to them', she instructed her daughter, in Somali. Fatima translated. Tugging her blue dress down over her knees, the young white woman trilled. 'Like birdsong,' she said. 'What does our English sound like to you?' Fatima translated again. Fatima's mother laughed, made a clanking swishing noise, and answered, 'Like a washing machine'. Later, when they had all finished eating and talking and watching a video of a parade of different groups dancing in Somalia, they said goodbye pretending to be birds and washing machines. When Fatima got married and moved away, the two women talked on the phone every few weeks or so for years, until the young white woman got married and moved out of the country and Fatima's number changed without warning.

She knew the scent of tar, sand and goldenrod that meant late summer, and the crisp, sour apple taste in the blue air that meant fall. She knew the map of the whole city. It mapped onto her chapped but strong hands, her feet, new scars on her knees, into her hair, her clothes. After all this, when she had to leave again and move thousands of miles away, she felt these ways of knowing tear, the way the white roots do when you peel a seedling from its pot, or threads do when you rip a seam apart. The map she knew by heart came away in shreds. In the new city, she got lost, only to find herself back at the same corner shop, with its dingy red off license sign and smell of beer, cumin, and newsprint. No one knew her name. No one recognized her style, those rubber and leather boots, or knew her to be useful for anything. She couldn't find a job and didn't know where to go to buy underwear, to find good seeds, even where to get decent peanut butter to make the homey comfort food of a PB&J sandwich. It rained, and rained, and rained. She felt as transparent as the windows of the house and the buses, the shops and the bus stops, shining and bleary with rain. It would take a long time to become visible or useful again.

Being Different

Fitting in

I wanted to fit in
but they said I'm ill-fitting.

The loners say I'm over-friendly
extroverts say I'm aloof.
The carnivores call me plant-based nut,
yet vegans call me carrion gut.
The eco-warriors call me gas-guzzler
the gas guzzlers call me tree-hugger

Black people say I'm white
White people call me brown
the Browns call me pasty,
pasties call me pie.
The able say I'm disabled
how awful it must be!
Then one lady said whatever I had
was not as bad as she.
Feminists say I'm oppressed
Extra-dressed call me floozy.

The locals call me foreign
but so do the foreigners.

The Sunnis call me Shia.
The Shia call me Sunni.
Traditionalists call me unorthodox
Alternatives call me paradox

Literalists say I'm heretic
Extremists think I'm terrorist
but terrorists call me sell-out.
I've been told to "get the hell out"
which I can't do before I "get the hell in"
so you can see what quandary I'm in!

All in all
flocks tell me
I don't fit in.
Maybe,
I won't fit in.
Maybe
It's unbefitting.

I raise my hands
which will betray me too,
the day forensics come around
investigating
leaves taken from books,
I know I have no chance
for no community
can hide my fingerprints.

Hands up…
I'm proudest when I'm middle of the road.
Fits like a glove.
I'm fallen in love with the squeezed middle.
Human, middle of the road, am I.
    Perfect fit. Hands down.

Being Different: Hair-raising

I had curly hair – the hair I was born with, the hair I have now – when the fashion was dead straight hair in a fringe, falling down the side like blinkers. I was deeply unfashionable. As a teenager in the 60s, it really mattered. Not so free!

No-one could pronounce my name – though it's quite straightforward. My (English) mother used to spell it out K-E-M for Mother-E-N for nuts-Y. Why did she choose N-nuts instead of n for November, n for Noddy, n for never. What was her subconscious saying?

By the time I was in my mid-teens I was proud of being half Hungarian. It felt exotic. I used to tell boyfriends, who were often prefects in my younger brothers' school. In the end my Father took me to one side and told me to keep it quiet because it was causing problems for my brothers. It wasn't so good for boys to be different.

My Father spoke perfect English, better than most native speakers. He looked Italian, dark hair, good looking. One Sunday he went into a country pub in the pouring rain and complained about the weather, as the English do. A woman turned to him and said

"If you don't like it, my man, you can go back to where you came from."

He was shaken – and so were we.

Childhood

My childhood was adventurous with good times and bad. I recall the first seven years of my life spent growing up on a council estate in Newport, where my family were the only black residents. Our arrival received a mixed reception and we experienced direct racism from an Irish family who lived opposite. Often racist insults would be hurled at us and we would be beaten up by our neighbours' children, all because of the colour of our skin which we were unable to change. My happiest memory was the closeness I shared with my older siblings. My brothers were very protective and always made sure we were kept safe.

Encountering Difference

Practice a smile
that warms like the sun.
Meet the eyes,
like the blue and white Niles.
Forget you are shy,
be a butterfly.
Pretend you are a queen
with a human face,
used to difference,
like a trusted friend.
Ask a question that draws her in.
Show your interest
in her every day.
Listen, hear, understand.
Make yourself vulnerable,
connect to what you share.

Translations

I imagined a drum and what it had meant,
In early films they'd used drums as language,
Every culture seems to have a drum,

Feel the vibrations through the ground,
How do you translate the sound,
How do you know what they're trying to say,
Do gentle sounds mean it's okay?

Deep bass sounds strong and hard,
Does it mean something's bad?
Is war on the horizon, or someone's on their way?
Is there an invasion or just music to play?

Is it encoded in the beats of our hearts?
Did we learn it from the past?
Did we pass our knowledge down through generations,
Or was it passed through DNA?

I hear my son, I know what it means to him,
To others especially next door his music is a sin,
I compare it to the warnings of war,
To my son his music is to adore!

Drums, bass and loud sound,
Has a way of connecting us through music,
Although each person has a different perspective,
Creating beats has proven to be inconclusive!

Oh Boy

Unmistakably malnourished I see a little boy lost, unable to express himself due to neglect. He gets himself ready for school without breakfast.

Teachers write to his parents and draw faces of the clock. Another reminder of the time the little boy should be in school.

A little boy lost, merely seven years in age, started staying out late with the older kids. Eventually one of the older kids' parents took the little boy lost into their home to stay. His parents had no idea of their son's whereabouts. Sometime the little boy would come home, "I'm staying just down the road". "What?" "Where?" or "Why?" – he wanted to hear. No questions asked. Out on a limb, this went on for years until the little boy lost was placed in foster care.

The little boy lost went in and out of foster care, which did little for his morale. Leaving school at 15 without any grades, he found solace and comfort in alcohol and cannabis, hoping the pain would go away.

The little boy lost is a father now and trying to turn his life around. He doesn't want his two little boys to be lost.

"Oh boy", you're such a brave young man now and yet, you still won't hear anything negative about your parents. Always helping others, a constant smile on your face, you're a child of God, you're meant to shine, as children should.

In the Head of a Stranger

So many different people,
So cold and rainy,
I find my eyes searching for others like me,
Some smile back.

I touch the buildings and trees,
They don't feel like home,
Where are the birds and lizards?
I'm actually missing mosquitos.

I take a deep, deep breath to smell home,
Deeper and deeper
I can't smell home,
I feel alone.

There is no gunfire here,
I am safe,
There is no war here,
Then why do I have to be braver than before?

Every new step I make I wonder.
I have to change a lot, everything.
As the harsh cold air hits my cheek,
I believe, I promise, I will not be weak.

A Sense of Place

Memories of Cardiff

The Rainbow Club was a favourite haunt of mine. A gigantic room thronging with noise, arguing, laughter and endless honkey tonk piano playing; activities too numerous to mention including a trip to the HTV studios to watch the filming of "Surrey with the fringe on top." Mr and Mrs Capener always appeared so patient in the midst of mayhem. I dreaded when he shouted out "all under elevens HOME – the real music was just about to begin.

Street Lamps Some children loved to make a rope sling, dangling down from the lamp post. They would sometimes put a cushion on the lower rope and swing, winding themselves one way and then another. I thought it was a pointless thing to do. I much preferred to add milk to an empty jar and shake it till it formed a ball, or drop down the canal wall after ringing the factory bell at Farnell's factory, pursued by the workers.

Home
Jack frost on the windows,
coal fires and helping my nana to clean the range,
coconut mats which were shaken daily.

A Sense of Place

The place where I grew up and played, the place of my childhood has gone, obliterated to such an extent that only in my mind's eye can I see the streets, the landmarks and the people.

The small terraced houses have been replaced, twice, with maisonettes then housing association dwellings. The narrow streets where we played 'Rounders', taking care to hit the ball down the street to avoid windows, or chased around, playing games like Ally Leego, are gone.

The tarmac roads that took the skin off your knees are gone, replaced with paving, pedestrianized streets and speed bumps, the lampposts where we hung our ropes to make a swing. Those tall sculptured pillars with arms sticking out designed, I thought, for the ropes to curl around, are gone, replaced by straight steel poles. No soft glow giving a hint of illumination but hard stark florescent light.

The old churches – grand affairs that were our stage, the sweep of steps designed, we thought, to be danced down – are demolished.

Farnell's wall, the division between the streets of Tiger Bay and the once imperial Glamorgan canal has gone. Farnell's wall a shortcut into a world of adventure and danger has all gone, gone now, along with the canal, the timber float and the docks.

Dredged and filled in to give the children a safe, sanitised, green place to play.

Are things better? The place has certainly changed. Yes the environment has improved, is safer and cleaner. Most have the latest household appliances and technological devices and of course inside toilets but still?

Back in the Bay

Back in the Bay I didn't realize how blessed we were,
how so many races in one place could occur.
I didn't know then, we were different,
living down the Docks on the seafront.

Our community was one in a million,
where down in the Docks, we all lived as one.
My friends were all kinds of races,
with parents who came from different places.

Our different religions and cultures were accepted,
everybody was definitely open minded,
although these times were taken for granted,
there wasn't anyone that couldn't be befriended.

Mrs Campbell became the first black headmistress,
none of those kids kept on with their badness,
Arab, Somali, Caribbean and Welsh,
just some of the origins all in a squelch.

Mount Stuart Primary I was so proud to attend,
we were protected from the outside world no end,
the teachers were attentive and taught with grace,
they didn't care that we didn't have a white face,

I treasure the memories of our freedom,
Break all the rules is what we done.
Brought home by the police,

My poor parents just wanted peace.

Playing in places that we didn't know were dangerous,
mud up to our necks and our hair a mess,
I am so glad that we made it, we didn't fail,
Because we're here today to tell the tale.

Grange Gardens

The Grange garden is in the centre of Grangetown. When I was a child this beautiful Green Park was the central meeting place for us to have our childhood adventures. As soon as we arrived home from school, we washed, ate and did our chores. Then we would plead with our parents to let us go to the park to play. The busiest time was between 4pm – 6pm when children from Grangetown would meet. We created dens, play fights, and even organised baseball and basketball matches. Children from all races would play peacefully together, and we took pride in keeping our park free from litter.

We built our dens with household items stolen from our homes, they were the places that were most private and hidden away from parents searching for their kids to return home. Arguments were settled in the dens and there was lots of laughter. Whenever I walk past this park, my childhood memories come alive. I watched the kids play and looked at the abandoned play things, no parents to keep order, toilets closed for years and the bowling green and the Park inn abandoned.

It seems that the recession has deprived Grange Gardens of its resources. But I still hold the park close to my heart. I sit down quietly read a book and wish my children played like we did.

About Cardiff

What do I think about Cardiff – so much, so many contradictions. It is my home, my history and has formed my character and the way I look at and judge other people. Cardiff has shown me the possibilities life has to offer and the difficulties of making the most of those opportunities.

Cardiff has shown me the good and the bad, the similarities and the differences between people. The way they live, and how choices have ramifications that travel unseen and unnoticed through generations.

Yet when I think of Cardiff and I think of institutional racism, of how good people with talent and intelligence have been prevented from reaching their full potential because of Cardiff's attitude to "Race"

I think of where Cardiff is situated within Wales, 10 minutes from the countryside or the sea and of how few local people use those resources. When I think about Cardiff, I think about Butetown – the Docks, its people. I think about and see Cardiff with those eyes. Cardiff for me is Butetown and Butetown is Cardiff – so much of what I think about Cardiff relates to its relationship with Butetown and the people who live there.

Lanes

My childhood upbringing was in Grangetown where every street was backed by a lane. Lanes were our safe haven. We would use the lanes to enter our friend's houses, without the prying eyes of our parents. Lanes were our playgrounds, where we settled disputes and sometimes fought with the bullies. We would walk through the lanes at night playing hide and seek and finding little treasures, such as lost coins. Today our lanes have been closed, shut off with gates by the council. They have become a place to dump rubbish and are never cleaned. Whenever I pass my lanes, I am overwhelmed by sadness and lost.

Identity, Womanhood, Connections

Sun

I look to the setting sun
I am a winner and won
I am a loser and lost
I am raging fire and frost
I am inactive in action
I am evolved evolution
shooting revolvers of revolution
within me.

I am the battle
between angel and demon,
soulful and soulless,
brave and gutless,
thinker and mindless,
guilty and sinless.

I am a loser at a loss
caught in the crossfire
of revolution within me.
Armies in combat
striving for civil coup
standing barefoot on coals of hell
while breathing heavenly.

I look to the rising sun
I hear the firing gun
My heart sinks
as daily mutiny for salvation

has begun.

I am the winner who lost
I am the loser who won.

Fighter

This is a part of my identity that has bought me a lot of trouble, which I would like to be rid of, but I don't think I ever can. What I have realised is that I can't and should not change this aspect of my identity but I should change the methods I use to fight.

Every element feeds into this aspect of who I am. I fight because as a Muslim justice, not only forms, but is the basis of our action. It is something Muslims should stand up for. However each occurrence of injustice is instigated or created in different ways and so it needs to be tackled by different means.

My identity as a Welsh Muslim feeds into this aspect of my identity. The Welsh, through history, have had to struggle for their country, territory and citizenship, all of which I can identify with. The Welsh have often been the underdog and I almost always find myself on the side of the underdog.

My relationships are the most important factor of my life. They include family and very close friends. I have a deep love and complete commitment to these relationships and would not tolerate anyone trying to harm them in any way. Hence the connection to the fighter – put another way, it is what brings out the fighter in me.

My history, which includes my place in Wales and Welsh history, is vast and goes back to the C7th. I have inherited Islamic history with which I have a further connection because my father's roots go back to the closest company of Prophet Muhammad, peace be upon him. Politics, too, permeates my history and holds great significance in my life and for my identity.

My Beloved

There will come days
You will hear accusations
despite innocence.
You will feel hate directed at you
in the name of love.
You will be viewed with suspicion.
I might be there with you
I might not.

My beloved son,
when that day comes
I wish to be your shield
pierced by arrows aimed at you.
I wish to take your pain
usurping it as my own.
I wish to take the poisoned chalice
and swallow the hatred that gushes
from those who don't know.
I wish to throw myself
from the plank you are forced to walk
and to give you the last breaths I have.
I wish to be the alchemist
who turns hatred into love for you.

But I cannot be any of these.
I am not vast as the sea
though my tears may seem to be
I am weak with nowhere to flee

from a treacherous world.
My beloved,
words are all the power I have
and they are all the power you have.

May they change hearts
and give hope to the hopeless
and convey a love that
is beyond words.
This is all I have.

I Always Knew

I always knew who I was and what I was. What I did not know was how I became the person I was at 16 years old.

I always knew that life was unfair and unequal but I didn't know why my life was the way it was. I always knew I loved in a white world but didn't know about the world.

I always knew that men ruled things and talked and discussed and took action, but I didn't know that women took the brunt of the discussions and actions.

At 18 I discovered politics. Black Power and I began to see why things were the way they were.

I had found the end of the thread that if I followed would lead me down the path of understanding and knowledge.

In politics I found my moral compass.

Teenage Years

As a teenager I was infatuated with Mills and Boons books which showed me expressions of love between two people. During my adolescence I observed my parents would never show affection towards each other in front of me and my siblings. One time my father was away for months at sea, and when he returned home, I thought my mum would run and fall into his arms. However she merely gave him a warm smile. Witnessing this made me think that I would not be doing this in my life when I settled down with a husband. Loving someone was going to be an important aspect in my life.

You called me "rag-head".

Thanks for your observations but I think you'll find "Highly ingenious Joyously Jocular Awesomely Beautifully Brilliant Effervescent Delightful Head" or the shorter HIJJABBED-head" much more accurate.

Experience of Being Different

My first experiences of racism, I recall, were when I was about five or six. I was not educated with the majority of my peers because I was a Catholic and was sent to be educated at a junior school in the town centre. All the children were white and I had never experienced this before.

On my first day at school the children started feeling my hair and before I knew it, they undid every single one of my tightly plaited rows of hair, because they wanted to see how it would feel, leaving me in a state of disarray and bewildered.

How Other People See Me

They can trust me
My word is my bond.
I sometimes have the annoying habit of looking elsewhere
when I am talking with them,
I only notice this because they turn to turn their heads
to see what I am looking at.
I look good for my age.
I do not suffer fools gladly
I stay up far too late at night
I am imaginative.
I do not drink enough alcohol
Some people are unsure of how to take me.

To Be or not To Be

They asked what I would be
if I could be what I wished to be.
I said "I would like to be a Be."
At first, they misunderstood me.
I said "not a bee, but a Be"
"Not a Do, Just a Be."

Not a buzzing bee.
Not a busy bee.
I just want to be an human Be
for I want to be me.
I want to be the best me that I can humbly be.
I want to Be me.
I'm already a queen bee.
I'm already as sweet as honey.
Now I just want to be a Be.
I just want to Be.

"We don't want your kind around," they said with their eyes, tones and words.

"Oh, I'm sorry that you don't want my kind a round … I know I've gained weight but I'm trying hard not to be a round. Actually I don't like me being a round either, I'd much prefer to be a slim, a tall, maybe an hourglass. I agree, definitely not a round.

But I'm sure you wouldn't mind my kind being a round if I was a merry-go-round".

… I said in my head many hours later.

Me

If I were big I would be a Garden of Eden
If I were an animal I would be a butterfly
If I were a fruit I would be an orange
If I were a vegetable I would be a runner bean
If I were a drink I would be Champagne in Paradise
If I were a circus I would be a lion
If I were a summer fair I would be a fairy
If I were wool I would be pure as the driven snow.

"Mother, mother, I wish you would ask about my whereabouts. Do you care enough? Where I've been and with whom?" "Don't back chat", you would shout. I'd sometime wonder: am I really your child? Most of the time I would secretly wish, please don't let it be true. I would let my mind wonder. Imagine a utopian family life, a mother who teaches her daughter right from wrong, teaches her about the changes in her life, as she grows up. You never taught me anything.

From childhood to my teenage years I wished that my parents were like my friends' mums and dads, like any other teenager's parents. I wished they would ask me: "Are you going to school today? Why aren't you in school? Have got any homework? Have you done it?"

After the summer holidays, my school uniform was old. I wished my mother would go with me to the shop to purchase a new one. Teachers at school kept asking me: when are you going to sort out your uniform. Things were not that simple. Dad had to go to work, leaving mum in charge of things and she was 'penny wise and pound foolish'. She didn't have a clue about how to budget Dad's wages.

The first thing she would do is go and spend them on trivial things.

One time I'd been to a friend house for tea and came home late. I wished they would say things like "you should have been home early." I felt abandoned and left to my own devices. I would be away all day and my mother wouldn't ask where I'd been or who with, or had had anything at all to eat.

Growing up a Girl

Hooya and Aboyo - When you told me stories about your upbringing I think you wanted mine to be the same. I obeyed and showed respect while my brothers did nothing. I cleaned and cooked without hesitation. Then late in the night I would stay up with a candle trying to finish my homework. My role was also to be a mum to my two younger siblings. I hated this and asked myself why they had to be born. I know you were preparing me for adult life but certain things should not have been part of my role. Girls and boys were different in my household boys would not cook and would made the kings of the castle. Girls were taught to obey without question and restrictions were placed in their everyday life. My bodyguards were my brothers, they reported my disobedience to the queen and king. Often I was said to be cheeky because I questioned their preference for the boys. Every day they would congregate in my house getting glamed up ready to dance the night away. I was confused and could not understand why.

I am a woman who keeps fresh mint
I am a woman who keeps paintings,
I am a woman who carries a mobile phone
I am a woman who carries keys
I am a woman who carries a pen
I am a woman who carries a handkerchief
I am a woman who wears a headscarf
I am a woman who wears dainty shoes,
I am woman who wears an elegant dress,
I am a woman who wears make-up
I am woman who loves the house that I live in.
I am a woman who loves painting
I am a woman who loves travelling
I am a woman who love dining out

Growing Up Different

If you are white in Britain, you do not grow up marked as different. You have the privilege of being treated as the norm. Yet as you grow up, you experience difference in many ways.

When I was a small child, my mother used to take me to church on Sundays. I watched as tall people in strange black robes and veiled heads greeted her. They would stretch out their hands to pat my curls as I hid behind my mother's coat. Were they strange men? Only later would I learn that they were nuns.

Difference is something that you learn to see and feel. As a seven-year-old, the teacher had us say where we were born. A Forces child, I was born in Hamburg. This was the 1950s, when Germans were still enemies. The taunts of "Gerry! Gerry!" followed me around the playground. I learned at an early age how it can hurt to be the other.

Sticks and Stones

She told me to say
"sticks and stones may break my bones
but names will never hurt me".
I repeated it, but it didn't ring true.
Words may not break bones
but they break hearts.

So when
my son said to me
that the words some say to him
upset him
though he knows
he shouldn't be a baby
they hurt him.
I didn't say anything
about sticks and stones
or breaking bones.

He didn't repeat the words
that hurt him so.
I felt my heart
break
into a million pieces.

I am a woman who keeps a
Quran
Prayer mat
Scarf
Hot water bottle.
I am a woman who carries
Tissues,
Tablets,
Prayer Mat
Purse and Mobile.

I am a woman who wears
Scarf
Heels
Dresses
Trousers

I am a woman who loves
Sun
My boys
Reading
Travelling.

They say meanings get lost in translation and that you can never really understand someone unless you walk in their shoes.

I ask you then, to take my hand and guide me to walk through your rib cage, so I can see how your heart beats. I ask you to allow me to navigate my way through the vault of your skull so I can crawl around the folds of your cerebral matter.

But I don't think we need to break any bony walls for me to know you, for the eyes are the windows to the soul and I have always been good at squeezing through even the smallest of windows.

I have already drowned in your tears before and somersaulted in your laughter, I have folded with shyness at your blushes and have floated in your smile. And many a night have I laid awake, restless and tortured in your snores, with no need for translation.

Roles

This is the world where we act out our roles.
We can play mother and daughter and we aim for our goals,
If we do a good job and we're told we can go far,
But what if I told you no matter what you do you're still a star?

As soon as we're born we are in character,
These lands and waters are here to charter,
Observing the obstacles that are in our way,
Trying to move mountains so everything will be okay.

We live again and again and again,
You have lived before some remember when,
Both joy and suffering we have all experienced,
With feelings like de ja vu situations are sensed,

Can't you feel it think about it it's not just me,
Everybody can feel it themselves everybody can see,
We've been here again playing many roles,
Learn, teach and rest with our very own souls.

I was there

I was there when it happened.
I was there
when you were shouted at by the headmistress
of the convent school.
She shouted in front of everyone
in the centre of the sports stadium.

I was there
when she claimed to be
an agent of God's anger,
condemning other mortals
to Hell;
God's love
forbidden for those whose sins
differed from her own.

I was there
when you thought God wouldn't forgive you
at fourteen
for not standing up for your beliefs,
for not being strong.
I was there
when you had to take off your hijab
in front of silent onlookers
on sports day.

And I was there when you came last in the race.
You couldn't see because your tears blurred your vision

and guilt was weighing you down pulling
your tracksuit bottoms down with it.
But you kept it together on the outside
even though you fell apart inside.
I was there
when you held up the royal blue track suit bottoms
and your head up high.
I was there.

I was there when you tried your best
to disappear into the darkness
because you didn't want anyone to see you.
I was there in the slow motion of it all.
I was there when you realised
that adults aren't always fair
or right and that even Christian nuns
can hate and be unkind and be unworthy of the name "Mary"
they take for themselves.

I was there
when you cried as soon as you got to the beige Honda
that had an issue with its carburetor and always stalled.
And when mum tried to console you.
And when she furiously fought your corner.
I was there when you never saw your friends again.
I was there when you had to join a new school
and the smelly teenage boys belched and cursed
using words you hadn't heard before.
I was there when you felt smaller than ever.

I was there when you cried yourself to sleep,
night after night,
night after night,
and you prayed for forgiveness.
I was there when you had dream one night.
Everyone said you were so blessed to have that dream.
I was there when they said you must be special.
That you must never forget the dream.

I was there
when,
at the age of thirty-four
you forgave her
and though you hoped she saw the error of her ways,
you knew she might not.
You forgave her anyway. You let it go anyway.
I was there.

The hurt disappeared.

I was there when you said
you wouldn't change any of it.
I was there
when you thanked God for keeping His promise
"With difficulty comes ease".

Baby Mothers

To all baby mothers who've been left on their own,
Get up smile and make a difference, coz you're not alone,
There's a whole world outside the door,
The options are endless, so don't be a bore.

If you get an idea that's in your head,
Don't ignore it, make steps towards it instead,
If you don't succeed at first,
Hopefully just trying will give you the thirst.

No more looking down on yourself,
That person in the mirror is your wealth,
You have the power to turn things around,
You will be shocked at the things you found.

Please don't isolate yourself,
It is time to get off the shelf,
Break free from the suffering and shame,
It's time for a whole new game.

In this game you only win,
If you think your losing just try again,
Things will change, you will be proud,
Proud of what you've accomplished you can shout it out loud!

I wonder

I have often wondered
how it would feel
to be normal, average, with the majority.
I wonder how it feels not to stand out
but disappear into the Bell curve of
    faith and
        mindset.

I wonder how it would feel
to be unnoticed,
raising no suspicion.
How wondrous it would be
to carry a rucksack into town
without people I pass running for cover.

I wonder how calming it would be
not to worry
whether I could protect my children
from hatred masquerading as freedom
from ignorance passed off as knowledge.

I wonder.

I wonder how it would feel
to be viewed neither with scorn
pity nor rejection.
To be with the masses
To agree.

To be an insider.
I wonder how refreshing it would be
to be able to sleep each night.

I wonder how it would be
to feel safe and carefree.

I wonder if such an existence exists.

But I wonder too
Indeed I am confused
How it is
that I can be a
minority, an outlier, an other,
different from anyone I know,
with thoughts and worries
that cross my mind alone yet
I too have a blessed and wonderful life
in an existence so temporary.
I wonder how standing out can be outstanding.

But it is.

Advice

Fantasy...

Life wasn't always fair to me,
So whenever I felt ill, I made up a fantasy,
When they told me I didn't have long to live,
I had to do something, I had to be creative.

I built a whole world inside my head,
When in reality I was really laying down in bed.
I chose not to ever get stressed,
That didn't always work but I know I'm blessed!

I learned fast to choose a different angle,
To be grateful, stay happy and soulful.
The combination has worked so far,
I have my family, house and my disability car!

I found out that when I'm in a hot climate,
All my symptoms go for definite,
So in my fantasy I'm in Barbados!
But here in reality I'm not even close,

I just need somewhere warm,
I don't mind a storm, chilling on a beach with family,
This is my fantasy!

It gets me through the rough days,
Beaches, kids, holiday replays, wishing all the while it was real,
Hoping that one day that's my deal!

I know better now

My sister and I decided to visit our former school, two years after leaving. We were so excited, flamboyantly dressed, floral trousers with pink tops platform sandals and heavy make-up.

'Let's hit the town' we thought. We felt on top of the world. Giggling through the staff car park, through the corridors and up the stairs, we knew just where to go. We did knock on the door though. In we went. The class full of rowdy kids went silent all of a sudden. We walked up to Mr Baldwin and told him we'd come to see him and the class. For a second he seemed astounded, perhaps he didn't know what to make of this sudden visit, but he soon composed himself and told class that we were former pupils.

Everyone was firing question at us 'What are you doing now?' 'Are you married?' 'How many kids do you have?' or 'Are you in college?' It was rather embarrassing. The thought occurred that we hadn't prepared for this. What did we expect? Mr Baldwin knew we were feeling uncomfortable, thanked us for the visit and wished us all the best.

I wanted to stay a bit longer, if only they would stop asking so many questions. Sullenly and quietly we walked out of the classroom, the school car park and the area.

I didn't leave the house for at least a week.

If I had to do it again, I would perhaps make sure either I'm in college or working full time before making any attempt at revisiting my school days.

Shimmering Shampoo

What gorgeous hair you've got said my teacher.
It's not a compliment I thought.
Do you colour your hair? Asked my teacher.
No!? I reply.
Light reflecting through the window, perhaps,
said my inner voice.

(Weeks later)

What type of shampoo do you wash your hair with? Asked my teacher.
Normal shampoo of course said my voice.
Here, I've got you this. It's gentle on the eyes and it's made of apples, it'll leave your beautiful hair shiny and soft said my teacher.

(Couple of days later)

Did you use the shampoo? Asked my teacher.
I felt ashamed for throwing it away because it stung my eyes.
Of course I did said my voice.
Little did I know, when lathering my hair I should have had my eyes closed, said my inner voice

(Afterthought . . .)

'Knowing what I know now you were a fantastic teacher showing concern about your pupil. Children hear and understand more than we think, but it's a pity I didn't understand much. I didn't fall into the category of 'little pitchers have big ears.'

Pressures & Expectations of Adulthood

If I took into consideration societies expectations of me being an 'adult of 50 years of age', in their eyes I would have 'failed'. I don't own my own house, not married, I'm not at the top of my career, don't go on holidays once or twice a year, no savings and I don't have a dog!

But for me I am enjoying my life, I have been through many trials and tribulations but I am still here standing strong. Too many people thing that they know what is best for me, dress a bit older, cut your locks, put on a bit of make-up, the list goes on. These things I always hear, but these are only material things. At this stage of my life I am thinking of what I can do to help others less than me. Contributing to the preservation of this planet earth, opening up my consciousness, looking beyond the physical and looking into the spiritual. Isn't adulthood all about thinking outside of the box, being independent, not letting commercialism and the tell lie vision (television), tell me what I should wear, what I should eat, what I should look like, where to shop etc etc.

Being happy and emotionally stable, learning from past mistakes. The only thing that really matters is the expectations I have for myself and the pressure I put on myself to achieve, my personal aims and objectives and what impact I can have on society and the lives I help to improve.

Memorable Moments & Objects

On Being Welsh?

Today was a special day. It was St David's Day and South Church Street School were taking part in the Cardiff Gymanfa Ganu – a singing-together-celebration, to be held in the Jackson Hall on Westgate Street.

I loved singing and dressing up, so excitement was high, bubbling up in my chest and making my feet tap and skip so that I couldn't stand still for my mother to dress me or to pin the large silver fake brooch to the shawl around my neck.

Mrs Lewis the teacher had told us about St David's Day and that it was held to celebrate the patron saint of Wales. We were all expected to wear the national costume of Wales, or our own national costumes. She understood, she said, that some of us or some of our parents were not Welsh, and we would be allowed to wear the national dress of our fathers. I relayed all of that information to my mother and asked her what I would wear.

Well you are Welsh, you were born here, and so was I and Nana so you'll wear a Welsh costume, said my mother. But my father wasn't born here. Can I wear his national costume? No he hasn't got one was the reply. Grandfer wasn't born here, can I wear his national costume, I pleaded. Grandfer was born in Jamaica but he was a British citizen and you'll wear the Welsh costume, was the final reply and the decision was made. It wasn't that I didn't want to wear a Welsh costume, it was just that the other national dresses were so much more colourful with bright soft fabrics and velvet cloaks. I could have fun wearing something like that.

St David's Day began damp and dark with a mean drizzle of rain that sneaked through your clothes, but did not dampen the excitement of the day. Take you partner's hands, get in line, stop talking and fidgeting, the instructions came thick and fast from Mr Chesconus the head master, Chester as we children called him. We marched out of school along South Church Street into Bute Road and across the bridge into town, bejewelled headdresses, long dresses and cloaks subdued by the light fall of rain. Curious onlookers stared with smiles on their faces or with curiosity, others looked then turned away quickly as though they were seeing something that was not true or should not be seen.

When we arrived at The Jackson Hall we had to queue, lining up tightly against the wall so as not, Chesconus said, to impede the progress of passers-by and we waited until we could go into the hall.

People smiled and looked, some said "good morning children" some said "Bora Da".

One group, two couples, stopped and looked at us all, then looked at me. "Have a look at her in a Welsh costume, she's not Welsh", "More like West Indian" said the other. I looked back, taught not to speak to strangers and not to give cheek to adults. Of course, I often did both but under the watchful eye of Chester I just looked back hard at them.

I <u>was</u> Welsh, I was born in Cardiff, sang Mae Hen Wlad Fy from memory.

Importantly my mother had told us, instilled in us that we were Welsh and now all of that was being questioned. It wasn't just what had been said, but the way in which it had been said. Spat out, spoken with derision and some malice.

I almost understood then, the way I perceived myself was not the same way in which others perceived me. What they saw was not all of me. That my sense of self must also be determined by people's understanding and acceptance of me as an individual.

Memory

"Ta Luv" – a warm feeling, another world, a previous life.

She's the only woman on the Tesco tills who speaks with a Cockney accent. Sometimes I choose that queue just to hear the familiar tones.

"Hang you on a minute." Did I really hear my mother's voice in a lino shop in Grangetown? The shopkeeper won't accept that he still has a Suffolk accent after a lifetime in Cardiff.

Phrases from another time, heavy with memories, conjuring feelings of warmth, of loss and belonging.

We are our memories, we are the stories that we tell ourselves and the stories that we've been told.

Being the young girl who refuses to be a servant, who aspires to learn and wishes for an education even as it is denied her. This is one of the stories my mother told me of her early years in the 1920s, stories that have helped make me who I am.

Then there are the stories I can tell of my own life, as I shape aspects of my past into narratives that take me to many different places and trace some of the routes by which I have become who I am, today, even as this journey continues.

Lost in Grangetown

I visited Grangetown quite a lot when I was younger, one of my aunties lived there and the dental clinic was on Cambridge Street, which I visited regularly because I had rotten teeth. I knew those parts of Grangetown and Penarth road where my aunty lived and the shops and the Ninian Cinema which we went to occasionally.

As Government policy had changed the way schools were configured and having failed the 11 plus exam, I had to leave South Church Street junior school and begin the September term in Grangetown Secondary Modern School, an old building which had had a variety of uses and names, most latterly Grange Council School, but was currently the place where 11 plus failures went and had newly acquired the presence of children from the Docks, aka Butetown.

During the summer holidays, before I was due to start at Grangetown Secondary Modern, my friend Philippa and I cycled across Clarence Road Bridge into Grangetown.

The idea was to have a look at the school before we started. We made our way down the lanes – a short cut Philippa knew – but very soon it became obvious that we were lost. Lost in Grangetown.

The terror and confusion. How would we get home and importantly what would our mothers say and do. Who could we approach for directions? We imagined everyone was looking at us and knew we should be there, if we only knew where "there" was.

Grangetown is about a mile from Tiger Bay/The Docks/Butetown where I lived. Grangetown in my 11th year was a predominately white working class area, with what I thought were very posh houses with Bay windows and front gardens.

Grangetown was not the same all over I discovered later when I had made friends at school, some of whom lived in small narrow streets of terraced houses not unlike those of the Docks. There was also a council estate built just after WW2 and a large derelict site known as "the site" waiting to be developed. This was much later to become Oakley Place.

I encountered some racism and name calling in and around school but generally got on well. I now live in Grangetown and have done so for the last 30 years and have watched the changes. Becoming less white and more mixed, or 'diverse' to use the latest euphemisms, with the arrival of Somali and Pakistani families. Of late the Eastern Europeans have arrived and it seems the old Grangetown families don't like the changes – it's a step too far. The Eastern Europeans are very different but look so familiar – look white but foreign.

Rusty

In the drive up to the house round the corner, the 1970s Nissan white rusted car, "Rusty", would squeal with joy much to the shame of the passengers, as the neighbours looked on. As we approached, the noise would get louder. We arrive at the gate. The name of my paternal grandfather is written on a plaque in beautiful Arabic calligraphy. My brother was given the same name because he was born within days following my grandfather's death.

My aunt opens the gates while my other aunt drives in, hoping not all the neighbours were awoken from their afternoon nap by Rusty. My uncle didn't drive because of his epilepsy which saved his life. I doubt there are many people as grateful to have epilepsy as my uncle. He didn't have to join the army of the oppressor. Not driving was the small price he had to pay.

Rusty was unwell, but good for her age, though getting increasingly rowdy as time went on. She was one of the few senior citizens to have air-conditioning. It was air-conditioning only when the car moved, with the temperature of the air being the same as the outside air. This is because it was the outside air coming in through small triangular windows that you can push out, apparently a selling feature. Had it not been for the seats being worn down to the metal underneath and the floor having holes that you could see through to the road, it might have actually sold. In the end, they kept her. I always imagined my grandfather driving in it, pipe hanging from his lips. They couldn't sell Rusty. We all knew that.

The rooms had changed around since my uncle got married. The front room was a massive library which the human and annelid bookworms could get their teeth into. The garden was where I spent most of my time during the day; I would spend many an hour caking myself in mud where the hose tap was often left dripping and forgotten. I used to build armies in the mud and it quickly dried solid at 40° C. It was hot but I did not care since there was no way I could do this clay modelling back in Cardiff. I might have felt differently had I known about the scorpions.

The birds would all gather to drink the water and you could hear them sing with joy that they were drinking, having been parched.

I read the classics in that house from *Vanity Fair* to *Animal Farm*. I slept everywhere. I slept on the roof in the summer to be awoken by the flies and cockerels. I slept on the floor. I slept in the bedrooms. I slept in the living rooms. I slept in the corridor. I slept in the garden.

My family wasn't the right sect for that area – they had twenty-four hours to leave, after a rifle was emptied outside the gate, indicating that they were no longer welcome – that was in 2006.

I never saw that house again.

They were lucky to have escaped with their lives.

Wash and Go

Wash and go shampoo and conditioner transports me back
to the shower in the house I never saw again.
The bathroom with pink tiles, with the drain in the middle
 of the floor, with the flush that won't flush
and had to be filled with water.
The bathroom with the lizards and cockroaches.
The bathroom that my father was sick in on his week visit back
after 40 years.
The bathroom where my late grandfather struggled
with his pancreatic cancer.
The bathroom that my late grandmother took her ablutions
one last time.
The bathroom that never had a lock.
The bathroom of the house they had to flee to save their lives.
Who could have known the power of this pistachio green liquid
that comes from the same coloured bottle? It was the first 2 in 1
shampoo/conditioner combination, yet with the one whiff
it transformed into a fragrant DeLorean.

Alive

Never felt more alive
than when I thought
I was to die
No cliché
that life flashed before my eyes
yet I could count my breaths
my heartbeat
my thoughts
all with Zen precision
I could control it
for a moment

A night in Paradise!

I drive towards the sound of the bass,
Windows opens to catch the cool night breeze,
As we get closer, we're met by the laughter of people,
The enjoyment of the air hits the atmosphere,

We are here and the smells amaze our senses,
It's dark yet the people and place are still full of colours,
We want to taste the food,
We have to taste the food!

We're in the moment that we want to save forever,
Enticed by the bass,
At the verge of joining in,
The dancing, the joy, the aroma of food all mingled up,

Pretty necklaces for sale,
Beach towels, lighters, magnets and T-shirts,
Gifts for the loved ones waiting back home,
We're touched in every sense.

Belief

Vagabond

My heart is a vagabond
yearning for home.
It is a traveller
with no fixed abode.
Avoiding capture of being bought and sold,
yearning to be slave to soul.

It is a stranger
looking for home,
it knows the truth
only the All-Knowing knows.
Truly
He knows
what its insides hold.

It longs for a future
with knowledge so bold
that

when it stops beating
it can return home.

About Growing Up

Growing up in Butetown, called Tiger Bay in my youth, I was surrounded by different cultures religions and family norms. My family was Christian – Pentecostal. I attended the Welcome Mission.

My friends were Muslim, Catholic, Christian and one Greek Orthodox and another of no discernible religion. I attended all of their religious establishments mostly for special occasions like Easter, Eid and Christmas midnight mass. I attended the Mission twice a week – Sunday and Mondays.

I enjoyed those days so much, joining in communion, singing and joy. I saw the peace and assurance the congregations gained and thought, there must be something in this. But each establishment, church or gathering showed the same levels of satisfaction from those who attended. Each different religious approach with their rites and rituals seemed all to have similar instructions and beliefs, the same fundamental truths and encouragement towards goodness and caring for others.

Because of that, because of seeing the similarities and not the differences, I do not believe in organised religion. I now consider myself to be a Humanist. I take on board as many of the teachings as I feel appropriate and, if I am honest, that I find useful.

I became politically active and my understanding of politics and society, especially within the framework of my own "community" led me to look at what and who I wanted to be – a humanist. Respecting the basis of most of the main religious groupings but opposing the way in which religion is used for the accumulation of wealth and power.

My culture is defined by my upbringing and the intervening years between childhood and now. My culture is in fact a bit of this and a bit of that based, within the context of Wales. Outsiders' assumptions about me, based on my culture are usually wrong. I am Afro-Welsh with a culture constructed by birth and life.

My mantra is "My ethnicity defines me but will not confine me" but I still enjoy a good session of hymn singing.

God Breezes

They flagrantly flaunt
their heavenly fragrance.
They're clearly Heaven sent.
I've sensed them.
You may say it's nonsense
but I'm Hell-bent
on smelling Heaven's scent
again.

That intense incense beyond dreams.
I never want to lose sense
of sensing the scents
and hence,
I made it my life sentence.
I know this sentence may not make sense.

Head in the musky clouds.
Forgive me for thinking aloud,
I wish they were common scents.
On Earth it's an aroma, travelling roamer,
never staying around long enough.
Please fragrantly flaunt yourself again,
Heaven scent, so Heaven sent.

God Breezes
I know you're there.
You take the away the pain-
    I'm waiting to greet you again.

Gratitude

I'm grateful for everything that's come my way,
It wasn't easy but that's okay.
Makes me extra grateful that we've come this far.
It's not coz of material things like my house and car.

Although, don't get me wrong, I'm grateful for them too,
I don't seem to have made it yet but I try hard at what I do,
I don't give up although things are so hard,
We've had many battles and yeah we're scared.

But we get back up, think about what we're grateful for again, and again!
And we learn to forget about the pain.
Our focus is reset and we learn the rest,
A positive angle on this great test, just try our best.

We have lots of chances and nothing is lost,
We always have choices no matter what they cost.
So I'm so grateful over and over,
Everything I wish to nurture!
Everyday I have been given another chance,
I guess this is my stance.

Grief & Loss

Peacock

She had five of the same porcelain peacocks. They were decorated with pastel colours defined with gold lines demarcating important features. One for each son.

Throughout the years she transferred them with her, country to country. Since she was living with us at the time, we had to keep ours on display.

It wasn't really my thing.

I had already lost the power struggle. We would still have silent battles for territory; one moment, when she was out of the living room, I would hide the peacock at the back of the display cabinet and slide a few of my prized possessions in front. I would turn my face and find the peacock had returned to centre-stage, as if it had walked there by itself. I could see a wry smile from the corner of my eye.

It's funny how territorial we women can get.

I often contemplated how other members of the animal kingdom resolve these disputes. Although an effective method of marking territory, I didn't think that spraying the house in a feline manner would be hygienic, especially since disputed land involved the kitchen. Despite possession being nine-tenths of the law and desperate times calling for desperate measures, I had to think of something else.

I would get days when I would see the golden peacock eyes and rage would kick in.

I hated that peacock. Really hated it. It would look at me, gloatingly victorious. Goading me. Mocking me.

Plots to exact bloody revenge shot through my mind. "Accidents happen". Porcelain breaks when "dropped" and subsequently "tripped over".

I never went through with it.

I find myself looking into the golden eyes now. They no longer gloat. Mourning has dulled their shine; it misses her too.

I don't know where the other four peacocks are. I assume somewhere in the backs of display cabinets across the world.

Our peacock has pride of place, centre-stage.

I passed through this corridor many times before

It was alive last night. It was filled with excited voices of my children and a sleepy grandma just woken. She kissed me on my cheeks and ushered me through. We tiptoed across the wooden floor after taking off our shoes, passing magnolia walls and the flip-flops on the side.

We went into the bedroom on the right to change the sheets on the double bed from pink to white. The boys refused to sleep on pink sheets. The boys had come to have a sleepover at their grandparent's flat which was around the corner from our house. They loved Friday nights. We arrived around 8pm which was early but actually later than grandma had expected. She thought we weren't coming, so she went to lie down. I was so sorry to wake her up. I said we could do it again tomorrow.

Turned out we couldn't.

The next night I tiptoed through into this corridor, my husband had rushed in a while before me. I saw his face. The paramedics had tried everything. He knew better than most, there was nothing they could do.

She was unconscious but her eyes were partly open. I could see the greyness that was rarely seen in Arab eyes and considered a sign of beauty.

She was taken out to the ambulance. Her husband (my father-in-law) stood in the living room as they had tried to resuscitate her. Silent.

The next time I saw her she was in a room in the ground floor of the emergency department. It was a white room, had strip lighting. I always hated strip lighting. She was on the bed facing Mecca. Her body was covered with a baby blue blanket and a white sheet.

I read her chapter thirty-six from the Koran.

I kept expecting her to sit up and talk to me, surprised at all the fuss and asking me if she had missed any phone-calls while she was out.

But she never did.

She never did.

That corridor is dark now.

Connecting to the World

"You don't understand" she sobbed.
It was true, I didn't. I didn't want to understand. I cried anyway.
There were waves of grief alongside gamma and UV rays;
they came gushing.
I was crying for my own inevitable loss; may be many years
from now, maybe not. She cried because of a raw pain
that hadn't quite reached me.
She was an orphan now.
The phone connected us. Waves of grief connected us.
Her mother was such a good woman.
My mother is a good woman.
We are all connected. We breathe the same air
ever since they cut the cord.
They cut the cord a long time ago.
That's when I cried for the first time after they held me
upside down and slapped my bottom.
The cold air hit me as well.
That was my first disconnect.
Since then, it has been a story of
disconnect-connect- reconnect- disconnect- connect-
disconnect.

Grief aside, it's the way of the world; so when the final
disconnect comes, I know I will reconnect properly with the One
who breathed life into me in the first place.

Writing

Pleasantly poetic

"It's pleasantly poetic
we're just not into poetry,"
they said to me
not knowing my heart had been ejected
painfully onto the page
scrutinised under a microscope,
subjected
to the whims and rejected
in the understatement age.

Being called "pleasantly poetic"
denied all the soul of my rhetoric.
It wished to be heard.
It yearned to be heard
and expressed as word.

But they called it "pleasantly poetic".
Heretic. They don't get it.

But I know
words can turn heads,
breathe life into the dead hearts of the heedless
and ignite sparks in the minds of the mindless.
Needless
to sell one's soul to resurrect others
but they named their crisis.
They'd already paid prices
denying moments so priceless;

when your heart skips a beat and your soul leaps
on hearing a word which turns your world
inside out
bringing your insides out.

About Writing

I've written notes, letters and short stories since I was able to write.

Writing has allowed me to express my thoughts and opinions in a buttoned down, children should be seen and not heard culture. To express anger and revenge in an atmosphere of repression and bottled up feelings.

My letters, to love ones to express the longing for reunion, to give the gossip and to complain to someone who was always on my side.

Writing for work, for formal consumption such as memos and minutes, briefings and ministerial's guidance and legislation – the conventions and restrictions on word usage and number.

What a joy to be part of a creative process, a creative writing class, where the only conventions are the style one choses to use and getting the 'Tense' right.

No restrictive word count only the restriction of time, time to write and time to hold that thought; that moment of clarity around what you wanted to say and how you were going to say it. The classes introduced possibilities and a chorus of other voices to be listened to, to join with, ignore or imitate.

To conjure memories and put them into word pictures others can see, can hear.

Penfold and Me

Penfold has been quite annoyed with me of late
He says I've been ignoring him.
It's true. Sad but true.
I have been ignoring him.
And avoiding him.

Penfold is my fountain pen. I had bought him when learning to write in my "tidy " book.
He has golden nib and a red, chunky plastic body.

We chatted about the situation the other day.
He said "You're ignoring me..."
Silence.
I stuttered a bit.
Then he said "It's ever since you've been using notes on that pansy, the iPad..."
I understood he was feeling a bit rejected, but then he started getting irate and shout-y.
It all got rather confrontational.

"No need for name calling" I said.
"What's he got that I haven't?" he demanded.
He was quite demanding.
I had to tread carefully.
And not answer the question.
 Definitely not answer the question.
It was time to take time out.

Once we had calmed and had time to think,
we were back to the drawing board.
I explained that he was my first love, and though,
as he himself admitted, he was rather temperamental,
he had helped me with my best work.
It could never be replicated. It was original.

He reminded me how inky words flow through him like blood
through veins and you could never get that with "the pansy".
He had a point; the soul flows through the pen,
you just can't get that with tablets or smart phones.
I didn't mention that there was an app and fonts for
handwriting though. Things would have got nasty.
Things were already messy after the confrontation.
There was ink shed. All over my hands.
I explained that it wasn't him, it was me.
I said that we should keep in touch.

We still get together every so often
but it's definitely awkward now.

Writing

In the beginning I wrote as a means to get all the stresses out of my head. Writing made all the pressures just melt away.

Then I met Karen Battle, she taught me that there were many other subjects to write about. The whole process of writing other than to cope felt like an uplifting healing process!

I wrote a book of poems, we had a launch alongside many others. Zainab invited me to this class and my writing went further and further into unknown realms.

Now writing isn't to distress or just a way to cope, now writing is magical and mystical. Reading other people's magic and hearing others people's magic is an honour. It's been an incredible journey!

Ideas and descriptive words jump into my head, all day long now, not just at night when I'm in my bed.

Words have become more powerful, more meaningful. I use them wisely when I speak compared to before.

I visualize the senses if I have a block – what did my eyes see? What do I hear? Or smell? What does it feel like? Did I taste it?

Writing and this class definitely opened up another world!

Thank you. (I still need help with spelling)!

It Bled

It bled.
It bled ink holier than blood of martyrs.
It bled words of years gone by.
It bled through scars they thought had healed.
Blue blood that runs through the pen so regal.

I have blue blood.
I have blue blood.

Blue blood for royalty in words that dignified us
as human beings.

The earth still spins around its own axis
and around the giver of light greater than it.
The ink that gave life to my thoughts
 and gave a microphone to my insides.
Richard of York gave battle In vain.
Blue is the battle – the battle that splattered blue blood
from veins as the heart beats.
Words speak of the battle; a bloody revolution within.
Civilisations started with ink. It links us with generations before.

The first fountain pen was given to the caliph of Egypt in 953
so he wouldn't get ink on his hands. But maybe it's meant to be
on the hands, for it runs from the hearts and minds to the
hands, bringing the insides out.

Free write about writing

She put her sandal on the table.

She told me to write.

"What the heck?" I thought. I couldn't write about a sandal! I didn't feel anything.

I wondered what I was doing here. I am scientifically trained. I'm a dental academic. What is the point?

But she was so enthusiastic and charming I just couldn't let her down. I thought I should put in some effort, for her sake. I loved her zeal instantly. What a gem!

Sadly, it was no use. I really tried hard. I could not think of anything to write and the room was a bit cold and I had struggled to park. I could hear the birds singing outside and the cars passing by. The clouds started making faces at me. One stuck out its tongue. A seagull aimed a missile at the wall behind the teacher.

Then, the faces from the black and white photos on the wall started to egg me on. "Write! Write! Write!" They were banging on the wall. They were stamping their feet. Those faces of the living and non-living were cheering me on. I think I saw them form a human pyramid and cheerleading act.

"Write, Girl, Write!" they chanted.

Then the sandal turned to me and mouthed its story, its rebellion, its rugged life, its love of all things rustic. It mourned how it was designed for sunnier climes. It started singing, "I am what I am". I think it might have been a bit tipsy; it was certainly out of key but sang with such gusto.

So I started writing.

And I found I couldn't stop.

Contributor's Notes

Abeer Ameer aka Abi B Da Hijjabi. Daughter, sister, wife, mum. Professional Tea Drinker. Loves God, Love, words, Cardiff and chocolate.

Alida Payson moved to Cardiff from America four years ago with her partner Eli. She loves to write, draw, explore new places and mess around in gardens. She is currently researching for her PhD in cultural studies and welcomed a new baby daughter this February.

Chris Weedon has been involved with Butetown History & Arts Centre since 1990 and she chaired the organisation for 16 years. She taught literary and cultural studies at Cardiff University for 34 years and has written widely on women's writing, gender, race, identity and culture. She loves to listen to people's stories and aspires to write them into history.

Gaynor Legall was born and raised in Tiger Bay, later to be called Butetown, to a mixed race mother and father from Belize, Central America. She has one daughter and later married an Irishman with two sons, they have two grandchildren, her extended family is diverse, multi-ethnic and multicultural. Gaynor likes people, eating and talking but not necessarily in that order.

Gill Gooden is a semi-retired mother of three and a grandmother. Gill has previously worked with people and trained as a social worker. She has enjoyed participating in the creative writing classes.

Marilyn Kemeny was a journalist who was involved in the anti-apartheid and trades union movements. She fought for equal opportunities and diversity. Recently she joined Women Making a Difference and returned to an earlier love of acting and theatre. She has a daughter, who makes her proud.

Pauline Andam was born in Cardiff and currently works for a homeless charity in the personnel department, she has two sons, loves working with older people and has a passion for Ghana, its people and culture.

Robina Samuddin was born and raised in Cardiff, by far the best city in the world to call home and home it is to her. She loves to travel, loves to study and read and is now beginning to love to write. Life's an adventure, never stop exploring, never.

Tasnim Hunt is originally from Bedfordshire England. She moved to Cardiff a few years ago. Tasnim loves writing and putting her thoughts onto the paper.

Yasmine Gulzar the youngest of four in a mixed raced family, father originally from Pakistan, mother from Penarth raised in The Docks, Cardiff often know as a cultural melting pot. Yaz started writing as a positive way of coping with heart disease and is eager to share her work!

Zainab Nur is a seamen's daughter who grew up in Cardiff. She enjoys meeting people and making a difference in people's lives. Zainab has worked in various roles in statutory local authority work but her new venture is developing creative projects which benefits communities. She enjoys reading and writing poems and feels that the writing workshop has given her confidence to continue further.

Facilitator's Notes

Christina Thatcher fell in love with Wales while studying for a Creative Writing MA at Cardiff University. Now, as a postgraduate tutor and researcher, she is passionate about understanding how creative writing can improve the lives of vulnerable people. Christina keeps busy off campus too by delivering community workshops, facilitating the local 'Roath Writers' group, hosting open mic events, and more. Christina's poetry has recently been published in *The London Magazine*, *Planet Magazine*, and the *Lampeter Review*, among others. To learn more about her work please feel free to visit her website: https://collectingwords.wordpress.com or follow her on Twitter @writetoempower.

Emma Beynon is a teacher and writer. She has an MA in Education from the University of Bath. In 2008 she developed the Write Team project, an innovative creative writing project managed by Bath Festivals. She works freelance teaching creative writing both in, and out of, doors. She currently works for Arts Alive Wales leading writing workshops for young people as part of their Caban Sgriblio Project: https://www.youtube.com/watch?v=Aq98xZpUTv4

Emma's travel writing has been published most recently in the Marine Quarterly and Yatching Monthly. She is currently writing a novel based on her sailing adventures in Svalbard. Forthcoming publications include chapters in *Making Poetry Happen* (Bloomsbury). You can find her on Twitter @writeoutside.